the ultimate guide to
successful
networking

CAROLE STONE
Britain's Networking Queen

Carole Stone was born in Maidstone, Kent in 1942. Her mother, Kathleen (always her best friend), and father, Harry (an ex-army boxer), ran a corner shop. Carole's older brother, Roger, was pathologically shy. It was while trying to help Roger out of his isolation that Carole first learned the value of friends and the need to network.

At school Carole was shy herself, but her mother encouraged her to think of being a journalist. After secretarial training Carole got a job as newsroom secretary at the BBC in Southampton. She went on to work for the BBC in Brighton and Bristol before becoming Producer of Radio 4's *Any Questions?* Here Carole learned the art of putting together very different people to produce lively and entertaining conversation.

In 1990 Carole left the BBC to freelance as a broadcaster, but soon found herself with a new career as a professional networker. Today, with over 22,000 friends and contacts on her database, she works as a media consultant, bringing together journalists, politicians and business people to discuss issues that interest them all. Carole is also a broadcaster and writer – well-known for her 'salons' and her huge Christmas party; there the confident and the shy, the young and the old, the famous and the unknown, mix, mingle – and network.

'Seize the moment and make the effort to get to know new people,' says Carole. 'As my mother always told me, don't be deterred by fear of failure, but be ready to look around the next corner of life, and face whatever is coming head on, knowing that you'll cope. That's the essence of networking.'

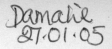

the ultimate guide to

successful networking

CAROLE STONE

LONDON

First published in the United Kingdom in 2004 by Vermilion, an imprint
of Ebury Press
Random House UK Ltd.
Random House
20 Vauxhall Bridge Road
London SW1V 2SA

Random House Australia (Pty) Limited
20 Alfred Street, Milsons Point, Sydney,
New South Wales 2061, Australia

Random House New Zealand Limited
18 Poland Road, Glenfield,
Auckland 10, New Zealand

Random House (Pty) Limited
Endulini, 5A Jubilee Road, Parktown 2193, South Africa

Random House UK Limited Reg. No. 954009
www.randomhouse.co.uk
Papers used by Vermilion are natural, recyclable products made from
wood grown in sustainable forests.

A CIP catalogue record is available for this book from the British
Library.

ISBN: 0091900255

Printed and bound in Great Britain by
Mackays of Chatham plc, Chatham, Kent

To my husband Richard – a reluctant networker

contents

acknowledgements

I would like to thank my editor at Random House, Fiona MacIntyre, and her assistant Julia Kellaway, for their enthusiasm and professionalism; together they have helped me distil the essence of all I've learned about 'good' networking.

Thanks, too, to Jonathan Lloyd of Curtis Brown, my agent, for looking out for me in the literary jungle.

I am also very glad – in retrospect, at least – that my journalist husband, Richard Lindley, cast a critical eye over what I was writing. I hope in return that I've helped him improve his own networking skills.

And to my family, and all the friends and contacts who have made networking for me so worthwhile and so much fun, I should like to say a very big and heartfelt 'thank you'.

introduction

I'm compulsive about people. I can't get enough of them. When I'm entering a room I fret if I pass someone who's leaving – I have to curb my natural instinct to stop them to find out who they are. Sometimes I just can't resist, and I hear myself saying my name, willing them to tell me theirs.

I admit this is extreme behaviour, and this book isn't trying to make you as obsessed with people as I am. What it *will* do, I hope, is give you the knowledge you need to become a normal, yet highly successful networker.

People have become my business, professionally and personally. I don't distinguish between the two. I love meeting people and bringing together those who otherwise might not meet – to me that's what successful networking is about.

Networking sometimes has a bad name – it can conjure up images of pushy people, ruthlessly brushing others aside to advance themselves socially or professionally. Some do. But to me the right kind of networking is making the most of the people you meet to your *mutual* benefit. Good networking – whether on a small or large scale, in your personal or working life – can be a rewarding experience;

something that will help you enjoy meeting people in any situation.

Today we are defined by the company we keep, much more than by where we were born or where we went to school. And we can keep the company of our choice to make our own networks.

This book gives practical advice to encourage you to become the best kind of successful networker: someone who shows a readiness to exchange ideas as well as business cards and social chit-chat; and, even more important, someone who demonstrates an interest in other people.

With this advice in mind, any worries about social or professional engagements looming ahead of you will be over. Once you can network in an easy way you'll find you get so much more enjoyment and value from the people you meet – so much more out of life.

1
basic principles

Q **Why should I show an interest in other people?**

A Because, quite understandably, people are flattered to be asked about themselves and begin to feel more at ease in your company. The more you are prepared to listen to their replies, the more you can expect them to like you and be interested in you in return.

It's a two-way deal. It's all about recognising that other people are very similar to you: they want to be liked, they want to have friends and to network – just as you do.

Q **How do I show an interest in other people?**

A By taking the trouble to ask them about themselves.

If you're not interested in other people now, don't think that you will suddenly, miraculously, *become* interested. You've got to work hard to make taking an interest in people your number one priority. It's all down to an attitude of mind and is fundamental to good networking.

Approach people wanting to learn something about them, and they'll respond. You'll have made that necessary contact that says 'I really want to know a bit about you'.

Q **What sort of questions do I ask someone when we first meet?**

A Simple, easy questions are best when you first meet someone. Try to keep in mind what makes *you* feel good when people ask you about yourself.

If you're at a social gathering start off with something like:

- *'How do you know our host?'*
- *'Do you live in this area?'*
- *'I was admiring your unusual handbag. I have a passion for them myself.'*
- *'Did you notice that wonderful portrait in the hall?'*

If you're at a business conference you could start with:

- *'Where have you had to travel from to get here?'*
- *'What made you decide to come to this conference?'*
- *'What did you think of the last speaker?'*
- *'Did you enjoy the session on internal communications?'*

And volunteer the same sort of basic information about yourself, and why you are there.

Q How do I ensure that I do the right amount of talking?

A
Just listen for a moment: in your conversation, who's doing all the talking? If it's you, stop, and ask a question instead. Try to draw out the person you're talking to.

Even if they're shy, everyone likes to be asked their opinion, to be made to feel important, to be the focus of attention.

Sometimes people just need to tell you something that matters to them – and it could be something of real interest to you.

Being a good listener goes a long way towards being a good networker.

Q **What are the right signals to send out?**

A Be the first to hold out your hand and introduce yourself if someone is hovering uncertainly nearby. You could say:

- *'I'm Mary Jo. I don't seem to know anyone here, do you?'*
- *'Come and join in our conversation, we're just talking about . . .'*

Body language is important. Have the hint of a smile on your lips – a look about you that shows you aim to enjoy the occasion and be friendly. People want to feel that any approach they make to you will be welcome.

Don't huddle together with others in an exclusive sort of way. Help someone new to join your group by making space for them.

Don't be unkind by shutting out someone who's trying to join in your conversation – shoulders can hurt feelings.

If someone is trying to talk to someone on the other side of you, make it easy for them: just move round them and pick up the conversation with someone else.

If you're reacting to a speech – or what's been said in conversation – with applause or a laugh, turn and involve someone near you with a smile.

Expect people to like you: if that's the signal you send out, the chances are they will.

Q What preparation can I do beforehand?

A Ignorance is not bliss when you're trying to get full value out of a networking opportunity. Whether it's the people or the issues they're discussing that matter, do a bit of research beforehand. Come armed with enough knowledge to join in an intelligent conversation.

If you're likely to meet an author, make sure you've read – or at least started reading – their book. You can ask where the idea for the book came from, or what the most difficult thing was about writing it.

If it's a business conference, get up to speed on the topic. If possible, get hold of a list of delegates in advance so you can pinpoint anyone you particularly want to meet. Ask for the CVs of the speakers so you know a bit about them. Use the internet too for your research.

Listen to the news or read a daily paper – keep in touch with what's going on in the world.

Don't stay silent just because you don't know *everything* about a subject – you can still make a useful contribution. But don't say you've read things when you haven't – you're bound to get found out!

Remember the basic principles:

- *Take an interest in other people – ask them to tell you a bit about themselves.*
- *Volunteer basic information about yourself.*
- *Be a good listener – it goes a long way towards being a good networker.*
- *Be the first to hold out your hand and introduce yourself when you meet new people.*
- *Expect people to like you: if that's the signal you send out then the chances are that they will.*
- *Do some homework before you attend an event so that you can join in an intelligent conversation.*

enter that room

– whether it's a social or professional occasion

Q What if I'm nervous?

A Take a deep breath and give yourself a sharp talking to. You're here, not where you would perhaps rather be – at home, in bed, at the movies – but here: just about to enter a roomful of people.

Make the most of it otherwise you're missing out twice – you're messing this up and you're still not where you'd rather be!

Don't worry about people noticing you're nervous at the beginning of an event: most people are. There's bound to be someone feeling exactly the same as you

Try to look at other people round the room in a way that encourages contact between you.

Remind yourself that your success or failure at this event is in your own hands. You're in charge. It's what *you* do that matters, not what other people say or do to you.

Tell yourself that you can leave when you want to. Give yourself a time limit, a minimum time you'll stay – say an hour, or whatever seems realistic without being rude. Then tell yourself that after that you can make your escape. There's no need to panic: you know there's an end in sight. Who knows, the chances are that you will want to stay longer than you ever thought you would . . .

Remember, nothing ever goes perfectly, so don't let a temporary setback deter you from your networking goals. We've all had a bad moment in the middle of a crowded room, it's how we move on from it that counts.

Q **What if people don't talk to me?**

A Talk to them. Grab a glass of something, then find the host or organiser and ask them to introduce you to a fellow guest. If there's no one in charge nearby, look for someone else on their own and introduce yourself:

- *'I'm Sue Brown, I don't seem to know anyone here, do you?'*

Keep in mind that there will be plenty of other people in the room feeling just as unsure as you.

Obey the three Cs: circulate, circulate, circulate. It's important that you meet as many people as you can – but you must make each encounter really count. A brief smile or a quick 'Hello!' and 'Goodbye!' is simply not enough. Give each person you meet your full attention for the time you're together. You'd like them to remember you so make sure you remember them.

Try to keep abreast of any subject in the news that could be a talking point. Books, films, television and radio programmes are also good talk material if the conversation is hard going:

- *'Have you managed to catch that wonderful new comedy series on BBC2 on Saturday evenings?'*
- *'What's your favourite TV soap – or do you hate them all?'*

Concentrate on your goal – networking. Don't be seduced into long cosy chats with people you already know well, but by all means meet up to discuss the event afterwards.

Promise yourself that you won't leave the room:

- *without having met the person you really want to meet;*
- *until you've spoken to someone who looks interesting.*

It's often the things we *don't* do that we end up regretting: the people we never said 'hello' to, the questions we never asked. Make sure that's not you, ever again.

Q **How do I join a group?**

A This can be tricky. If the group's in deep, animated conversation, wait for a pause, then introduce yourself briefly:

◆ *'I'm Carole Field; hope I'm not barging in . . .'*

Nod and smile to anyone in the group you recognise.

Try not to bring everything to a halt. Let the conversation continue and don't interrupt the flow of words for more than a moment.

At a natural break in the chat, give the group a one-liner about yourself – how you know the host:

◆ *'I'm Sue Brown, I met Yvonne through her book club.'*

or why you're here:

◆ *'I've come because I want to learn more about personal safety.'*

or ask a question or make a comment:

◆ *'I was sorry I missed Gordon Smith's lecture. Was he good?'*

You're networking!

Q **How do I tactfully leave a group?**

A It's important not to get stuck in a group for any longer than you want. Explain that you have to catch someone before they leave:

▶ *'I've so enjoyed talking to you, but do excuse me, I must catch John before he rushes away.'*

or that you're looking out for a friend joining you:

▶ *'I promised to be by the door when my guest arrives. Will you excuse me.'*

And then you can slip easily away.

A friend of mine always picks up two glasses of wine when she arrives at a party: that way she has a ready-made reason to move on – to deliver that other glass she promised to get for a friend.

Q **How do I leave a single person?**

A The essence of good networking is to give the other person your full attention when you're with them, but then to move on.

If you're talking to just one other person, this takes diplomacy: you must leave them gracefully. It's not only rude, it's not good networking to leave someone stranded on their own. Next time you meet, they may remember their experience and you'll be the one to find yourself abandoned.

You have a choice: suggest they join you in going over to meet someone new, or draw someone else into your conversation. Once you've done that, you're free to leave.

If you find someone insists on sticking to you all the time whatever you do, then just say you need a private word with one of the guests, and leave them behind – with somebody else of course.

Q **What information should I put on my contact card?**

A Contact cards are the lifeblood of a successful networker. A card needs no more than your name, e-mail address and mobile telephone number, but you can include your business or private address if you want to.

Have your contact cards to hand so they are instantly available. (I've seen people lose the will to live while someone digs ever deeper into their handbag or jacket pocket!) I've bought myself a little case for my cards, so I always know where they are. Whatever you do, don't leave your cards in a briefcase or bag in the cloakroom.

Q **Who should I give my contact card to?**

A Hand over your card to anyone who asks for it, or anyone you want to remember your name. But don't dish out your contact cards at random: people should feel special if you offer them your card.

Do make sure you get a card back from anyone you want to keep in touch with. If someone has no card, hand them yours and suggest they send you their details later; but if you particularly want to keep in touch, scribble down their telephone number or e-mail address – that way you leave with the information you want.

Make sure you always carry a pen that works and a small notepad or at least a piece of paper.

Q **How do I keep track of the people I'm meeting?**

A When handed a contact card, try to jot down on the back of it:

- *where you met*
- *some distinguishing feature*
- *who they were with*
- *the topic of your conversation*
- *anything that helps when, weeks later, you're trying to put a face to that name*

Q **Is it best to stand up or sit down?**

A Unless you're really weak at the knees, don't sit down at a drinks party or reception, however tempting it is.

Standing, you're far less likely to get stuck with one person – and much more likely to meet other people. Remember, it's all about circulating, so keep moving!

Q **Is it best to circulate solo?**

A Yes. If you arrive with a friend, separate at the door and compare notes later.

Even if you come with your partner, circulate alone. But by all means bring your partner over to meet people you've found interesting.

Don't take the easy option and huddle in a corner gossiping to the person you came with: that way you'll meet nobody new. People you don't know are much more likely to approach you if you're on your own.

Q What do I do if I need a break?

A Don't let yourself flag – cue the cloakroom visit and a chance to recharge your batteries.

But remember:

- *you're never off networking duty – even in the loo*
- *you could meet someone interesting while checking your hair or straightening your tie*
- *stay tuned at all times*

Q **There's someone I especially want to meet – how do I make it happen?**

A Do your best to find someone to introduce you personally. What matters here is *who* makes that introduction: this may determine how seriously your quarry will take you. So try to be introduced by someone they know well or admire – you could perhaps set this up with a mutual friend the day before if you know both people will be at the event.

Then it's over to you to grab your target's attention. Give a firm handshake, be friendly and brief in what you have to say:

♦ *'I've read all your books, and found your latest one the most intriguing of all. The main character has just got to be based on someone you know really well.'*

If you can't get help, you must hover and wait for the chance to introduce yourself. Hold out your hand, state your name clearly, and say why you're there, and why you want to meet them:

♦ *'I'm Tony Smith. I'm so pleased to have the chance of a quick word: I've a marketing idea I think could be of interest to you.'*

Hand over your contact card and ask for the best way of contacting them in the next day or two. That way the power is left in your hands to follow-through.

Do make sure you keep it brief. Don't try to make a full-blown pitch there and then in a crowded room.

Q **What if I don't manage to talk to the person I really wanted to meet?**

A If, despite your best efforts, you didn't manage to make contact with the one person you needed to speak to, all is not lost. Adopt damage limitation:

- *confirm that the person was actually at the event*
- *ask the host or the organiser for their contact details*
- *get in touch the next day: 'I think we were both at the same party/conference yesterday. I was sorry to miss you because . . .'*

Then you can suggest a meeting, arrange to send your proposal or even make your pitch briefly there and then.

Q **How do I make my mark and ensure people remember I was in that room?**

A If you're at a conference or seminar, try to ask a relevant question or make a comment from the floor; but if you do, keep it short and make your point clearly.

Never be known as someone who opens their mouth on every occasion, whether or not they've got anything worth saying. On the other hand, don't leave wishing you had said something, but were too nervous to do it. It's a question of kicking yourself into action at the time, rather than kicking yourself later.

Stay alert and follow conversations closely. Don't let your mind wander just because what's being said doesn't immediately grab you. If there's a particular issue being discussed in a group, try to have a viewpoint and say something pertinent, whether it's a serious or light-hearted topic.

If it's a professional gathering, listen carefully to what's being said by the speakers and make a point of having a word with one or two of them in the break period:

♦ *'I'm Mary Jones. I run my own coaching company. I was very interested in what you had to say about self-development.'*

Q **What if I forget someone's name?**

A It's so easy to forget a name – particularly if two people you know as a couple appear separately, or you meet someone outside their normal setting.

If you're in a group, you can try to busk it by introducing the someone whose name you've forgotten to somebody else you do know:

● *'This is John Smith . . .'*

and just hope the other person responds with:

● *'And I'm Bill Brown.'*

It often works. If it doesn't, you'll just have to own up:

● *'I know your face so well, but after saying "hello" to so many people this evening, I've just for the moment forgotten your name. I'm so sorry.'*

Don't, in any circumstances, let this person move on without first finding out their name. If you do then you've lost the chance to renew what could turn out to be a useful contact.

Q **What if I'm snubbed?**

A Occasionally I've had a curt or unhelpful response when I've introduced myself to someone. A dedicated networker has to take that chance. I've usually forgotten about it the next day.

Don't dwell on what looks like a snub. And don't let the fear of a snub stop you from 'working the room'.

If someone does snub you, give them the benefit of the doubt. Maybe:

- *they were distracted*
- *they were anxious to be on their way*
- *they were just a bit clumsy in their response*
- *they realise they were rude to you and now regret it*
- *you didn't hear them correctly*

Say 'hello' to them again if your paths cross and you could find their response is altogether different.

Q **How do I respond to a snub that was definitely meant?**

A If you feel sure that a slight was intended, then respond – if necessary in front of those who've heard the snub:

- *To someone who obviously thinks they're better informed than you:*
  'Do you really think so?' plus a condescending smile.
  Nothing more – just wander off.
- *To a sarcastic comment on what you're wearing:*
  'This outfit's had so many compliments today, I think it can cope with that.'
- *To a petty, inconsequential snub:*
  'I'm so glad you've got that off your chest . . .'
- *To an obnoxious snub:*
  'Are you always as rude as that?'
- *To a hurtful, unnecessary snub:*
  'What satisfaction has that given you?'
- *If the snub has a grain of truth:*
  'You've got a point, but I think you could have made it without being so offensive.' And then off you trot.

If you're sure you've been snubbed by a friend or colleague, take it up with them the next day and say you'd like an explanation.

Don't let a snub continue to fester: forget it or sort it out.

Q · What final checks should I carry out before leaving an event?

A

'Can we go now?' I hear my husband Richard say – some people are reluctant networkers. But before saying 'yes', I insist on making a networking check.

You must make sure:

- *that you've spoken to anyone you particularly wanted to meet*
- *that you're clutching two or three contact cards*
- *that you've scribbled down the odd note to remind you to follow-through*

Now you're free to leave.

Find and thank the host – that's important.

Make a clean getaway. Don't linger, blocking the entry hall and saying endless 'goodbyes' to people you've already spoken to. Just go.

When you enter that room:

- *Remind yourself that your success or failure is in your hands: it's what you do that matters, not what people say or do to you.*
- *Don't panic: set yourself a minimum time that you'll stay – and then make the most of the occasion.*
- *Circulate, circulate, circulate.*
- *Have your contact cards easily to hand and make sure you ask for the details of anyone you'd like to stay in touch with.*
- *Don't leave the room without meeting the person you really wanted to speak to.*
- *Make a note of anything you promise to do for someone and make sure you do it.*

3
follow-through

Q **What do I do with the contacts I've made?**

A You're back at base, you've done your best. But don't put your feet up quite yet. It's now that the real work begins. It's no good – having worked that room, met those people, shaken those hands – forgetting most of what was said and promised.

Translate those hurriedly written notes into something you'll be able to read in the future. You must do this as soon as you can, on the same day if possible, otherwise there's a danger you'll be unable to decipher what you've scribbled down.

Q How can I make sure I do all I've promised?

A Keep your legible notes on your desk and tick off the tasks one by one as you tackle them:

- *follow-up with a promised call*
- *send information requested*
- *order a book or DVD that's been highly recommended*

Q **Where should I keep people's details?**

A Make it a priority to transfer all the contact details on the cards you've collected to your electronic database or address book. It's important to double-check for any notes you may have made on the back of the cards and cross-reference each new entry with where you met:

- *'Met at Pauline Reid's birthday party June 2004, interested in meeting again.' Then put a note under Pauline's entry that you met this new person at her party.*
- *Who introduced you – 'Great friend of Tony Wood; says he's a lover of wine and an expert on education.'*
- *Any additional information that will make you remember them – 'Wearing pink tie; Tuesdays best day for lunch.'*
- *Note the name, if known, of any partner (and whether married or not), children or business colleagues.*

Now, if you want to invite the new contact somewhere, you can if you wish include a partner and the people who put you together – or at least let them know that you have followed-through their introduction.

Q **Should I put personal comments by my entries?**

A Do put a short comment such as 'very friendly, good fun!' or – to help you remember them – 'very tall, dark curly hair'. But don't store comments that could be embarrassing if seen by other people – 'groper'; 'boring'; 'to be avoided' – you can never be quite sure when someone, or their friend, could be looking over your shoulder at your address book or computer!

Q **What other information is worth making a note of?**

A You can have a way of noting if you think you might want to invite someone to a future event (I have a little box to tick on any name in my electronic database). Then if you decide to hold a party of your own later on, you can quickly bring up a list of all those people you've met recently and want to meet again.

You can also store people in your database in a way that makes it easy to 'call up' anyone interested in a particular subject or from a certain area: yoga devotees or people who have a home in France.

Q **Is it really important for my notes to be 100% accurate?**

A Make no mistake: accuracy is very important. Don't be sloppy – that's unprofessional, and not good networking practice. To avoid upsetting people, make sure you have:

- *made a note of people's titles*
- *made a note of any letters before or after their name*
- *noted if they've got an honour – they'll want you to get it right*
- *got the spelling right (people are always forgetting the 'e' in my name, Carole)*
- *got the postcode right*
- *listed mobile numbers and e-mail addresses*

When you've done all this, throw away the contact cards you collected. But do try to keep a back-up copy of your database or address book – you can't let all that networking go to waste!

Q **How do I renew a business contact I've made?**

A The best way is to get to know your contact's secretary or PA.
Don't try to by-pass the gatekeepers. Make sure you get their
correct name and title too. They can give you access to their
boss or make it extremely difficult for you ever to talk to them.
Make sure you:

♦ *ask for their help in having a word or making an*
  appointment
♦ *give them as much information as you can about yourself*
  and what your approach is about – it's only natural
  courtesy

Finally, do make sure you keep the information you've
collected updated. When someone you haven't heard from
recently makes contact, just check you have their latest
details.

Q **What should I do once I've entered the contacts on my database?**

A As you enter these new people on your database, go through the conversation you had in case there was anything you promised to do, in addition to the notes you made at the time. This is an essential element in good networking, and it really pays off handsomely.

A networker must be known as someone who can be relied on, a serious player. It's something people will really notice about you. People so much appreciate it when you remember to do something you promised, rather than just letting it fall through the slats of life. That way you'll gain a reputation for following-through.

To be recommended by others as reliable is good for business *and* for friendship.

Q **What if someone asks me for details of one of my contacts?**

A Be generous with your contacts. You don't have to give out personal details – not all your contacts would like that – just an office number, e-mail address or the name of the PA will do.

Or say that you are happy to forward a letter or an e-mail to the person concerned.

If you're generous in this way, people are much more likely to be helpful to you in return.

To follow-through successfully it's important that you:

- *Transfer details from the contact cards you've collected to your address book.*
- *Make sure you're accurate with people's details – titles, honours, correct spelling.*
- *Make a list of anything you've promised to do – and do it.*
- *Be generous with your contacts.*
- *Remember the secretary or PA is the gate keeper for your access to their boss – keep them fully informed.*
- *Regularly check that your address book details are up-to-date.*

4

the hostess
with the mostess:
the good host

– at lunch, dinner or a small drinks party

Q **How many people should I invite to a lunch or dinner?**

A Six people round a table is fine if it's important that everybody should be involved in the same conversation. But for networking I prefer eight or 10. That gives your guests a better opportunity to meet new people.

For a small sit-down meal like this, I always try to tell my guests in advance who else I expect to be there and what their interests are – it may alert them to good topics of conversation.

Q **How many people should I invite to a drinks party?**

A Fifteen to 30 is a good networking number for a drinks party but, like the airlines, overbook. However well-intentioned, people drop out on the day. It's far better to squeeze people in than have too few of them rattle round an empty room.

Conversation flows much better when the joint is jumping, the room abuzz with talk and laughter. It makes networking so much easier for your guests.

Q How can I make sure people will actually come?

A Send out formal invitations about three weeks beforehand. For a more casual gathering, use e-mail or ring people about two weeks ahead.

Include an RSVP with your address, your e-mail or your telephone number for people to get back to you. People are very bad at replying to invitations, but don't be discouraged – they don't usually mean to be rude.

For a formal lunch or dinner, it's important you know who's coming, so if you get no reply don't hesitate to ring up to find out if your guests can make it. Have someone in mind you know would not be offended by being asked to come at the last minute – just in case one of your guests drops out.

For a party, if there is someone you particularly hope will come who has not replied, it's quite acceptable to contact them a week or so before the event to double-check that they received your invitation.

I usually give a call or drop an e-mail two or three days before the event to anyone I haven't heard from, something like:

♦ *'I suspect you're away at the moment, but just checking that you got my invitation for Sunday. I do hope you can make it.'*

Make it easy for people to leave it 'open' as long as possible if they are trying to juggle dates or baby-sitters. Pressure is not good networking and people will say 'no' if you force them to give an answer too early.

Q What does my invitation need to say?

A For a lunch or dinner say '12.30 for 1pm', or '7.30 for 8pm' – whatever suits you. Then people know when they really have to be there if they're not going to be rude. But do be prepared for people who arrive a little early!

For an early evening party, put the start and finish time on your invitation. I think one-and-a-half to two hours is the maximum for this kind of do – say 6–7.30pm or 6.30–8.30pm.

However, for a birthday or other special occasion party that will probably continue late, just give a start time – say from 8pm. If there's going to be food, say 'buffet' or 'supper', or whatever it's going to be.

Please *don't* invite people to an 'all-day' party – 'Just drop in any time'. Your guests are bound to miss the people they really wanted to meet or see again, and those who stay around the whole day are unlikely to be worth meeting by the end of it!

Q **Is it a good idea to have a wide mix of guests?**

A Yes indeed. Be brave: mix young with old; those at the top of their profession with young people on the first step of their career; business colleagues with friends.

Don't hold back from inviting people from as many different worlds and age groups as you can. All but the stuffiest people are usually pleased to meet others not in their own circle.

Q **Can I ask people I know have quarrelled?**

A For a party, don't worry if you know particular people have fallen out with each other; they could well appreciate the chance to make up on your neutral ground. But don't invite sworn enemies to the same small lunch or dinner party without making sure they're happy about it.

Q **What food should I serve?**

A For an early evening drinks party I skip food altogether, or at most provide bowls of nuts and crisps – most people will be going on to eat elsewhere.

For a party that will go on late into the evening, you will need to provide substantial snacks or a buffet. If it's 'finger food' make sure it doesn't fall apart when you pick it up. If it's a buffet then make sure it can be eaten with just a fork, and keep it simple: something cold is easiest.

Prepare everything in advance. Get your friends or relatives to help you hand the food round or encourage people to help themselves.

For a lunch or dinner party remember:

♦ *Your guests have come to see you and meet your other guests, rather than just to eat. Don't get hung up on food – that's not the most important thing.*

♦ *You don't have to be a great cook to be a good hostess, but, whatever you cook, prepare as much as possible in advance. On the day, you must be with your guests, not in the kitchen.*

Of course, caterers do leave you free to give all your attention to your guests, but I think they can spoil the friendly atmosphere you want to create. I much prefer to manage the food and drink, either on my own or with the help of a trusted friend or two.

Q **What about drinks?**

A I stick to white and red wine plus mineral water, but if you know some of your guests will want a lager instead then get some in. Make sure you've chilled the white wine, water and any lager.

You'll find some guests are kind enough to come bearing bottles of wine. Some will taste delicious, others will be horrible. Say a warm 'thank you' and put these generous gifts aside for another day. Go on serving your own wine: otherwise people will find themselves drinking all sorts of different brews that may not mix at all well.

To avoid any shouts of: 'What do I have to do to get a drink around here?' make sure there's a plentiful supply of whatever you're serving, and that glasses are regularly topped up. It's a good idea to enlist the help of a partner, good friend or someone who is looking a bit on their own, to make sure the glasses are constantly full.

I leave my guests to decide how much they drink. But if someone's had more than enough, and is maybe causing trouble, then I try to find a reliable colleague who can see them safely home, or at least into a taxi.

Q **Must I greet all the guests personally?**

A Yes, this is very important. Try to make sure it is you who is there to welcome your guests when they arrive. If that's not possible, make sure you have a trusted friend who is prepared to stand by the door and welcome people on your behalf. No one wants to be confronted by a stranger on the doorstep.

Your guests may be slightly nervous, especially if they don't know you well. By putting your guests at ease from the start, saying how pleased you are to see them, you'll get them in the mood to enjoy meeting each other.

Make sure you, or someone you ask to listen out for you, can hear and answer your phone. People may be ringing to check directions or to ask if they can bring a friend at the last minute.

Q **How do I help my guests to network at a drinks party?**

A Circulate as soon as the majority of people have arrived.

Half-way through the party you could say a word of welcome to all your guests together:

- *'I just want to thank you all for coming this evening. I'm sure there are many of my guests who don't know each other, and I may not have time to introduce you all. It will give me such pleasure if you lend me a helping hand by introducing yourselves to anyone you don't know.'*

This just sets the scene for people to feel free to meet and talk.

But, where possible, introduce your guests to each other with a helpful line that will give them a chance to start a conversation:

- *'This is Mary, we met at the yoga class last month.'*
- *'This is Bill, it turns out we go to the same gym.'*
- *'This is Cathy, we're members of the same city networking group.'*

Keep your eye on your guests – if someone looks bored or left out of the loop, be helpful and bring them in to the conversation:

- *'Mary, have you told Tom about the golf tournament you won last week?'*
- *'Bill, did I tell you that Kate has set up her own public relations company?'*

Make sure any VIP guests are not isolated because people are too shy to talk to them or don't want to look 'pushy'.

But do stop any of your 'stars' from being monopolised – you can tell if that's happening by their hunted look. Gently interrupt to say there is someone they just must meet before they go, and lead them away.

Q **How do I help my guests to network during lunch or dinner?**

A When you sit down to eat, make sure everyone knows who they are sitting next to.

A round table is ideal for networking because there's less chance of anyone being left out of the conversation. Someone sitting at the end of a rectangular table can sometimes find themselves out of the loop for a time: it helps if you can have two people sitting at each end.

If the moment looks right early on, say a general welcome to your guests around the table.

Speak to the person on one side of you over the starter and to the person on the other side over the main course. If you can, make sure all three of you join in the same conversation at some point. Throughout the meal, make sure there is no one around the table without anybody to speak to. If there is, either include them in your conversation if they are near enough, or make sure they are drawn into one next to them.

It's important that all your guests get the chance to talk to each other. Have a seating plan in mind, but be prepared to alter it if you find those you had planned to put next to each other have already talked themselves out over the pre-meal drinks.

Swap places with your partner or a good friend after the main course, just before you serve the pudding. It refreshes the conversation around the table.

If there are lots of you at a big table then get, say, all the men to move a couple of places to the left, so that everyone has someone new to speak to.

If the conversation is flagging, introduce a topic that's in the news. This can be good for bringing everyone together, but don't force it on people.

After the meal, suggest that any of your guests who have not yet had the chance to chat sit next to each other over coffee.

Q **What if I have something I particularly want to speak to certain guests about?**

A Before your guests arrive, make a note of anything you particularly want to say to anyone:

- *to congratulate them on something*
- *to ask them for information*
- *to return something you've borrowed*
- *to invite them to some other event or a movie*

If you can, sneak a quick glance at your notes from time to time, to make sure you've said what you want to say to particular people.

For a drinks gathering, it may not be possible to tick people off your list as they arrive, but as soon as the party is over, check your list for those who said they'd be there but didn't show. Contact them the next day to make sure they're okay. Also follow-up on anyone who didn't reply to your invitation – maybe you have incorrect contact details.

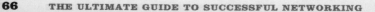

Q **What if one guest starts to monopolise my attention?**

A Your guest could well be asking you for information or a favour – or may be wanting to invite you to a future event. Make a note at the time if it's particularly important to you.

However, it's quite acceptable to ask if your guest could contact you the next day with their request, when you've more time to talk.

Q How do I get people to leave?

A I usually carry on serving drinks up to half-an-hour after the finish time. By then most people have begun to make a move.

If you really want people to leave because you're going on somewhere else, just move about the room saying: 'I have so enjoyed your being here, sorry I have to draw the evening to a close, hope to see you again soon.'

Q **What do I do when it's over?**

A Wash up when you like, but before you go to bed that night, do make sure you've made a note of anything you have promised to do for any of your guests.

Remember, that's the mark of a real networking host.

As a good host you must:

- *Tell your guests in advance what time your event will start and what time it is likely to finish.*
- *Be brave and invite a wide mix of guests.*
- *Greet your guests personally – they need to be put at ease from the moment they arrive.*
- *Remember you are there to help your guests meet each other, so be with them rather than in the kitchen.*
- *Make sure white wine, lager or mineral water is chilled – and keep those glasses constantly full.*
- *Introduce your guests with a helpful one-liner to ease them into a conversation.*

5
the good guest

– at lunch, dinner or a small drinks party

Q **Should I ask who else is coming?**

A For a small lunch or dinner party, don't ask who else is coming unless you know the host very well indeed. A good host will tell you anyway, but you don't want it to look as if accepting or refusing an invitation depends on who else is invited.

Q **What can I do to help my host?**

A Try not to arrive with a look that says: 'I'm here, entertain me.' Be ready to meet – and enjoy meeting – the other guests.

Don't plonk yourself down in a corner to gossip exclusively to an old friend.

If your host looks flustered, or you feel a bit lost yourself, offer to refill people's glasses.

Don't be the guest who arrives, gazes round the room to identify the most 'important' people and then tries to monopolise them. If you meet a 'star', have a good chat, but don't hang in there unfairly – other people want to meet 'stars' too.

Q **How much should I drink?**

A You know best how drink affects you, so stick to what you know you can handle. If you don't usually drink, then stick to one glass.

Try not to 'steady your nerves' with a drink before you arrive.

Make sure you drink plenty of water along with the alcohol.

Drinking too much means you won't make a good impression and you won't remember whom you met – the very opposite of good networking.

Q **What should I talk about with people I don't know?**

A Small talk should be your secret weapon. Until you know a bit more about someone, it's best not to start in with a rant about religion or politics or anything else that can arouse strong passions. Your aim is not to offend people unnecessarily.

Don't be afraid to start with a compliment:

- *'I couldn't help noticing that stunning brooch'*
- *'Where did you get that sun tan?'*

Small talk is a wonderful way of testing the waters, easing into a conversation and gradually finding out a little about the other person.

People who say they don't have time for small talk usually have no big talk worth hearing.

Q **What are the best topics for small talk?**

A Holidays are a safe topic, or try a film or television programme you've seen and can say something interesting about.

Talk about your work in general terms, but don't go into details about your job if they're really only of interest to someone in exactly the same line of work.

Feel free to talk to other people about their profession in general terms:

- *'Have we got the right sort of judges?'*
- *'What's really wrong with the National Health Service?'*
- *'Do you think we're all working too long hours?'*

Q **What should I avoid talking about?**

A Small talk doesn't mean tedious talk. Avoid boring people with the saga of you and your builders, or your failed attempts to control your acne. Everyone has quite enough of these tiresome problems of their own to deal with.

Never, however tempted, ask at a social gathering for free professional advice if you find yourself talking to, say, a lawyer or a doctor. Remember – they're off-duty and there to relax; they certainly don't want to know about your divorce or prostate problem. If you really want to consult them, ask for their office number and give them a call the next day.

Q **What is good conversation?**

A Good conversation is inclusive – a subject that everyone in the group can at least have a view on, if not in-depth knowledge.

In good conversation, the topic changes every now and then in favour of someone else in the group who has a particular interest in the new theme. You can try to pick up a cue from the previous conversation:

● *'That reminds me Paul, what was it you were saying earlier about that new project you're working on?'*

Or simply say:

● *'Sue – are you the one who's about to move to Scotland?'*

Q **What if I think I've snubbed someone?**

A If you think you have unintentionally snubbed or been rude to someone, or promised to have a word later with someone at a gathering and then failed to do so, make sure you contact them the very next day to explain and apologise.

Act quickly, or it could sour your relationship and dent your reputation as a good friend and networker.

Q **What feedback should I give my host?**

A When you write or phone to thank your host, let them know whom you met and liked at their gathering. After all, you were invited so you could meet other people.

Tell your host of any particularly interesting conversations that took place. For a host, that's half the fun of it.

Q **Should I return the hospitality?**

A Yes, do try to keep a note of the people to whom you owe hospitality. Entertain them in return or invite them to an evening out you feel they would enjoy. This continues the networking circle.

Q **What is the definition of a good guest?**

A A good guest is much sought after: someone who enters into the spirit of the occasion, has something to say, but is also prepared to listen.

A good guest appreciates the effort made by the host and is happy to help wherever they can – perhaps by talking to someone who is particularly young or shy or looks a bit 'out of it'.

A good guest says 'thank you' and will be asked again – to do more networking.

As a good guest you should:

- *Arrive ready to enjoy meeting the other guests.*
- *Be prepared to help the host re-fill glasses or hand round food.*
- *Include anyone who looks lost or on their own in the conversation.*
- *Remember that small talk is your secret weapon – it can lead to big talk.*
- *Return hospitality at a later date.*
- *Send a thank-you note or ring to say how enjoyable the gathering was – and mention anyone who made a particular impression.*

6

run your own networking 'salon'

Q **How do I keep in touch with people I've met recently?**

A Hold your own 'salon!'

A salon is a great way of bringing together new contacts and long-term friends, colleagues and relatives.

It could be a 'political' or 'literary' salon or, like mine, just a salon for people I like and want to introduce to my other friends.

The important thing is that your salon is on the same day of the week, at the same time, in the same place for a series of, say, six weeks (if weekly) or six months (if monthly).

The salon can be held in your home, in a room in the office where you work, in the boardroom of a large company or in the private room of a pub near your job.

If it's for people at work, then your salon could be at lunch time, or after work one evening. If you're holding your salon at home, then Sunday morning coffee or a midweek tea party may be a better bet.

How long should a salon last?

A   The salon should last long enough for people to have a chance of meeting most of the other people there. If it goes on too long, some people will have come and gone before others arrive.

An hour-and-a-half is about the right length of time for a social networking event like this. I run my salon on a weekday from 6–7.30pm in my flat-cum-office.

Q **How many people should I invite?**

A It doesn't really matter if there are just half-a-dozen of you or a large crowd – a salon is simply an excellent way of taking a chance encounter on to the next stage.

Q **Who should come to my salon?**

A The whole purpose of a salon is to bring together different kinds of people. Mix your personal friends with your business colleagues – and one or two of your family if you think they'd enjoy being there.

If it's a work-based networking group, but meeting outside the office, don't be worried about inviting people from rival companies. There's always something you can learn from each other: contacts to make, career advice to exchange.

Suggest your guests bring a friend or colleague. Extending your salon to 'friends of friends' increases your own network and is an easy way of meeting new people.

You could extend your salon by inviting a speaker to come and talk to you. It doesn't have to be an important person – just someone with something interesting to say. Authors, for example, are often pleased to come and talk about their latest book. Or if your salon is being held at work, invite one of the company managers to talk about a relevant subject.

Invite anyone you know who is particularly bubbly and good company to join you occasionally.

You will gradually get to know which guests are fun, engaging, have interesting things to say and yet are prepared to listen. Hang on to these people; they are the precious product of good networking.

Q **How do I let people know about my salon?**

A By word of mouth, or you can ring or send a note to anyone you would particularly like to be there, setting out the dates of your series of salons.

Q **What should I serve?**

A If it's early evening, serve a chilled, inexpensive, but non-headache-making, white wine, and mineral water.

If you're meeting in a private room above a pub, you may be able to get the room free, provided your guests use the cash bar. This means that though you'll have the work of getting your salon together, you shouldn't have to pay for the drink.

It really is not at all necessary to serve food.

Q **How do I help my guests to network?**

A As at a drinks party, try to introduce your guests to each other with a helpful one-liner:

- *'This is Jo, we share the same accountant.'*
- *'This is Bill, he has just arrived in London from Birmingham.'*

About half-an-hour after people start to arrive, say a word of welcome to the assembled guests. Stress that you want your guests to meet people they don't know and to leave with at least one new contact card – in other words, to network.

For your salon to work:

- *It must be on the same day of the week, at the same time, in the same place, for a series of, say, six – weekly or monthly.*
- *Let people know about your salon by word of mouth or ring or send a note to anyone you would particularly like to be there.*
- *Make sure your guests know the start and finish times of your salon – ideally it should last for one-and-a-half hours, or two hours maximum.*
- *Over-book – however well-intentioned, people always drop out on the day.*
- *Encourage your friends to bring a friend or colleague to your salon – but ask them to let you know their name and a bit about them beforehand.*
- *Help your guests to meet each other and make it clear that this is the purpose of your salon.*

7
network on!

Q **How do I widen my networking circle?**

A Join as many organisations as you have time for – and not only those directly connected with your business or main interest. It's worth trying something different such as a book reading group or a cinema club.

Accept invitations to other people's events, even if you're not sure it will be of direct interest to you. You never know whom you might meet, so if you've got the time, go along . . .

Investigate any new group you hear about that you think would attract other people in your age group or with similar interests. It could be a think tank, a political party, a business group or just a group of people wanting to meet regularly to exchange ideas.

Go along to any debates, lectures or seminars you see advertised that sound intriguing.

But don't just go for the main event, as my husband does. Make sure you arrive in time to talk to people beforehand and then stay on for a drink afterwards – and network.

Q **What reasons can I give for bringing people together?**

A There are all sorts of ways to encourage networking. A dog-loving friend of mine says that for months she had just nodded politely to others walking their dogs in the park. One day, on an impulse, she introduced herself as each passed by, and invited them to call in for coffee the following Sunday morning. Four turned up that week. She did the same thing the following month. This time there were eight, and two of them brought a friend.

This sort of get-together can come from any group of people you know with a common interest. All it needs is an informal invitation to say that you will be in a certain place at a certain time – only one person need come to make it worthwhile. Again, you're networking.

Q　**How do I nurture my new contacts?**

A　Networking is much easier if you have something in your diary you can invite your new contacts to. This is where the salon is so useful. Or it could be a group you belong to where you can take guests, or some exhibition or show you already plan to go to. This is the next step you take after meeting someone, before you know them well enough to invite them to lunch or dinner.

Keep a note of dates that are important to your friends and contacts:

- *birthdays*
- *an exam result*
- *a hospital check-up*
- *a job interview*

Just a note or call on the day can make all the difference to someone.

Q **How involved should I become in people's personal concerns?**

A Respond if you hear someone has had a bit of bad luck; and do congratulate people on their triumphs, even the small ones.

Be a good listener to a colleague or friend in trouble, but try not to take sides in quarrels about personal relationships – the chances are your friends will make up and you will have lost one of them!

Be an honest colleague and friend – but don't be too blunt. Try to listen, be tactful and be there when you're needed. You will need your friends throughout your life: don't say hurtful things, in a temper, that you will regret.

Q **How big should my network become?**

A If, like me, you want to build up a large network of colleagues and friends, then you soon will. But I know how hard it can be to keep in touch with all of them, all the time. So don't be too hard on yourself. Accept that you'll make contacts and friends and then, through your networking, make more. But while some will become very close to you – friends for ever perhaps – others will move in and out of your life quite naturally.

Make sure you give networking a good name:

- *Always be ready to meet someone new.*
- *Be interested in other people.*
- *Don't be possessive – share your contacts.*
- *Keep your relationships in good repair – nurture your network.*
- *Accept people for what they are – nobody's perfect.*
- *Network your friends and colleagues – and watch them benefit.*

conclusion

I won't say that successful networking is easy. It takes that extra effort to be sure you're always ready to meet new people and then to develop those contacts.

Throughout your life you'll be meeting people in different situations. Being a good networker simply means making the most of the people you do meet – whether for pleasure or business.

It's so satisfying to know that something has come of that chance encounter because you took the trouble not to let the moment slip by. You'll get to know people whose company you enjoy and who can open up opportunities that you would never have thought of before.

Successful networking is exciting and rewarding: it's well worth the effort – you never know where it may lead . . .